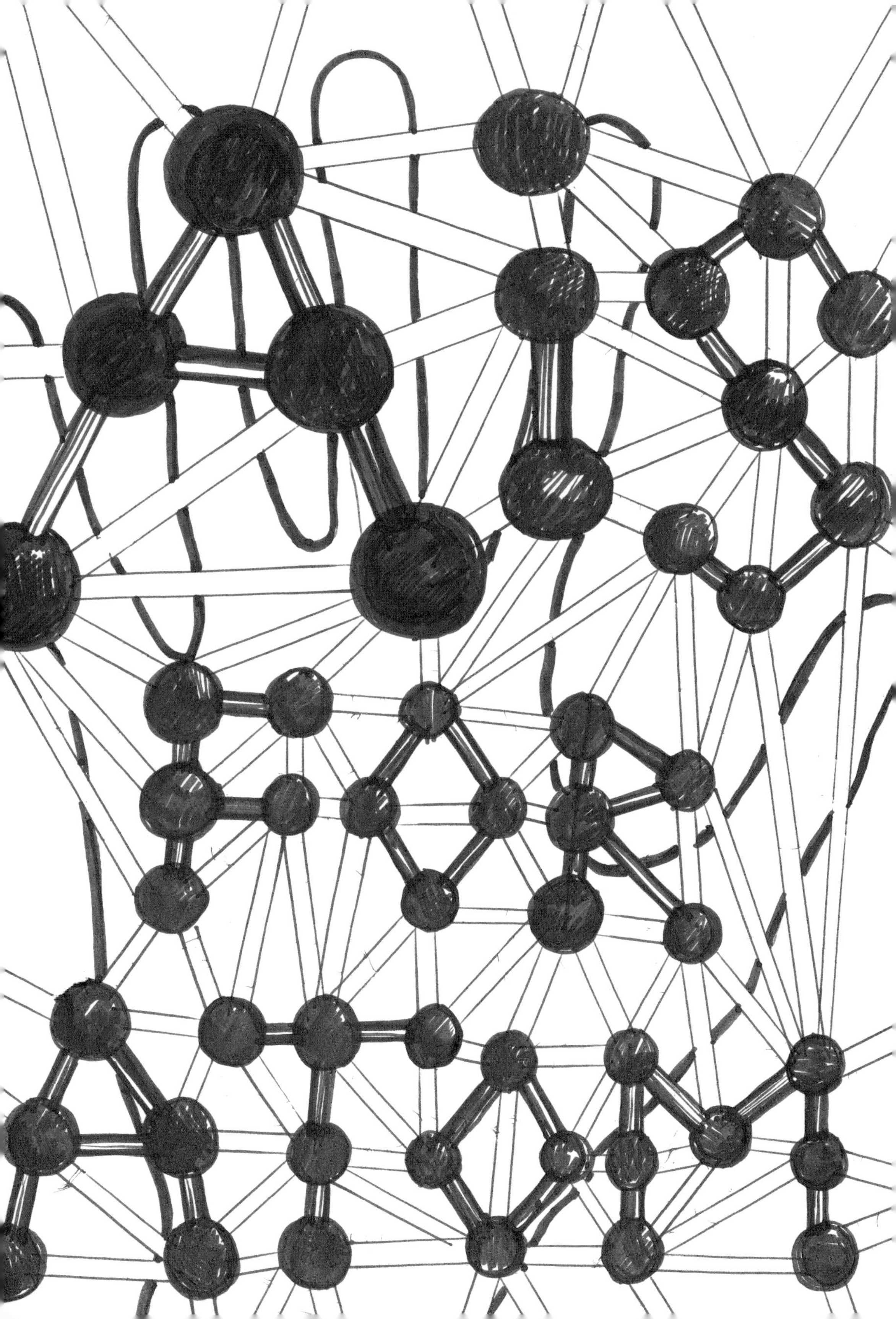

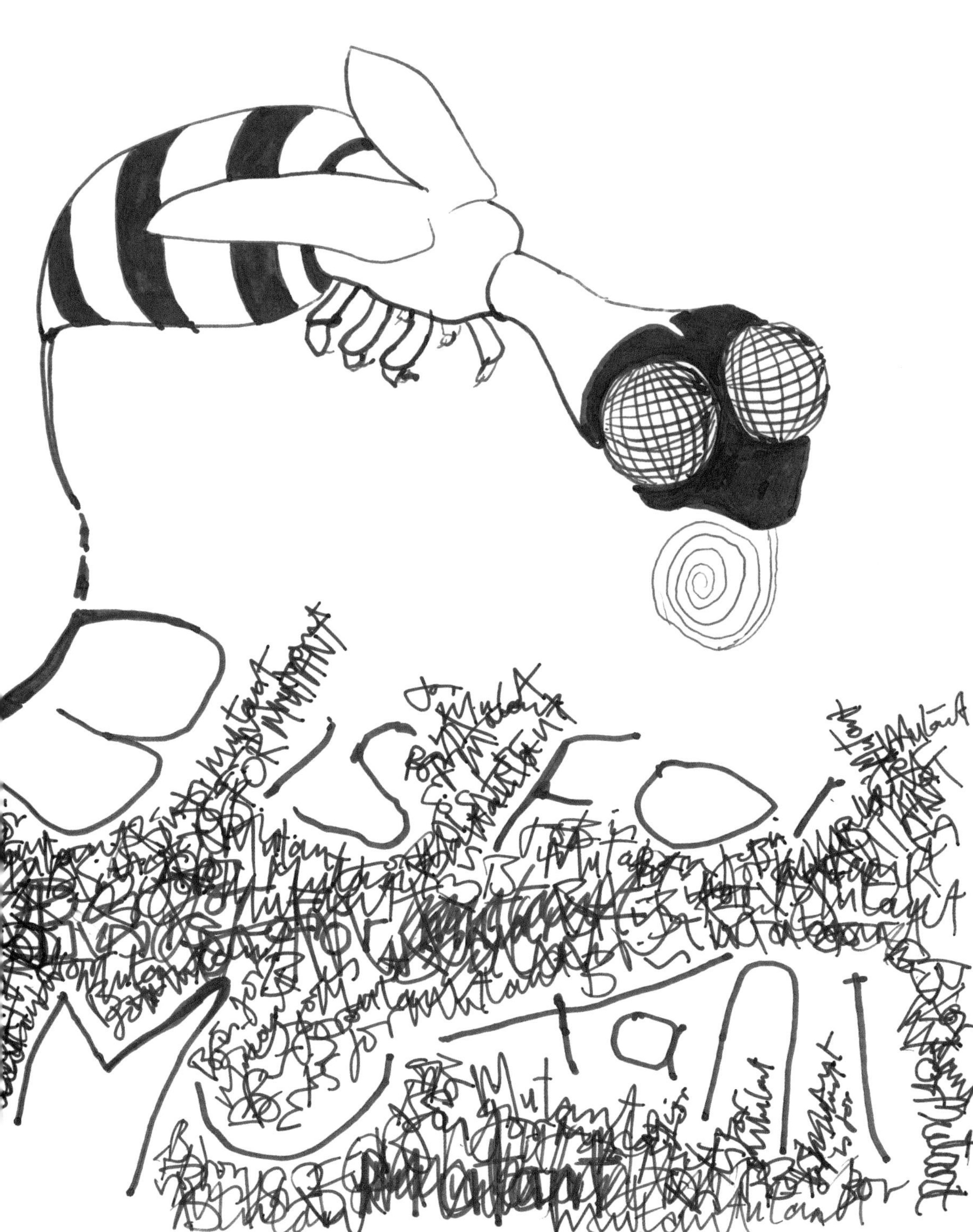

MUSEO
MUTANT
FOR MUTANT
Mutant

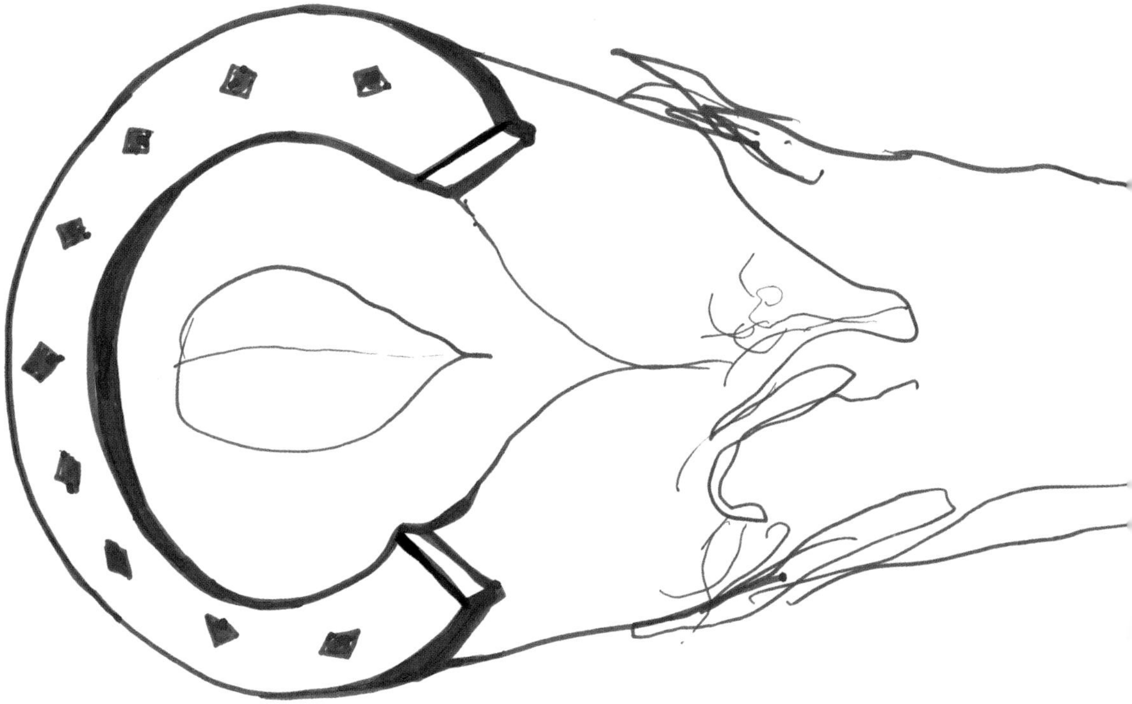

is forever

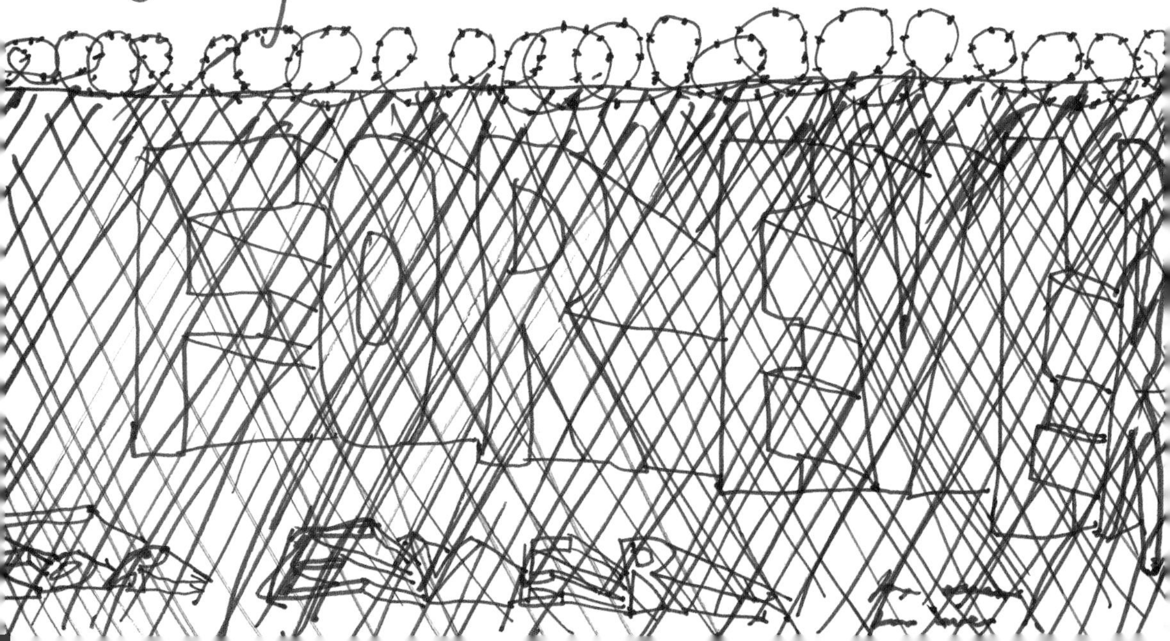

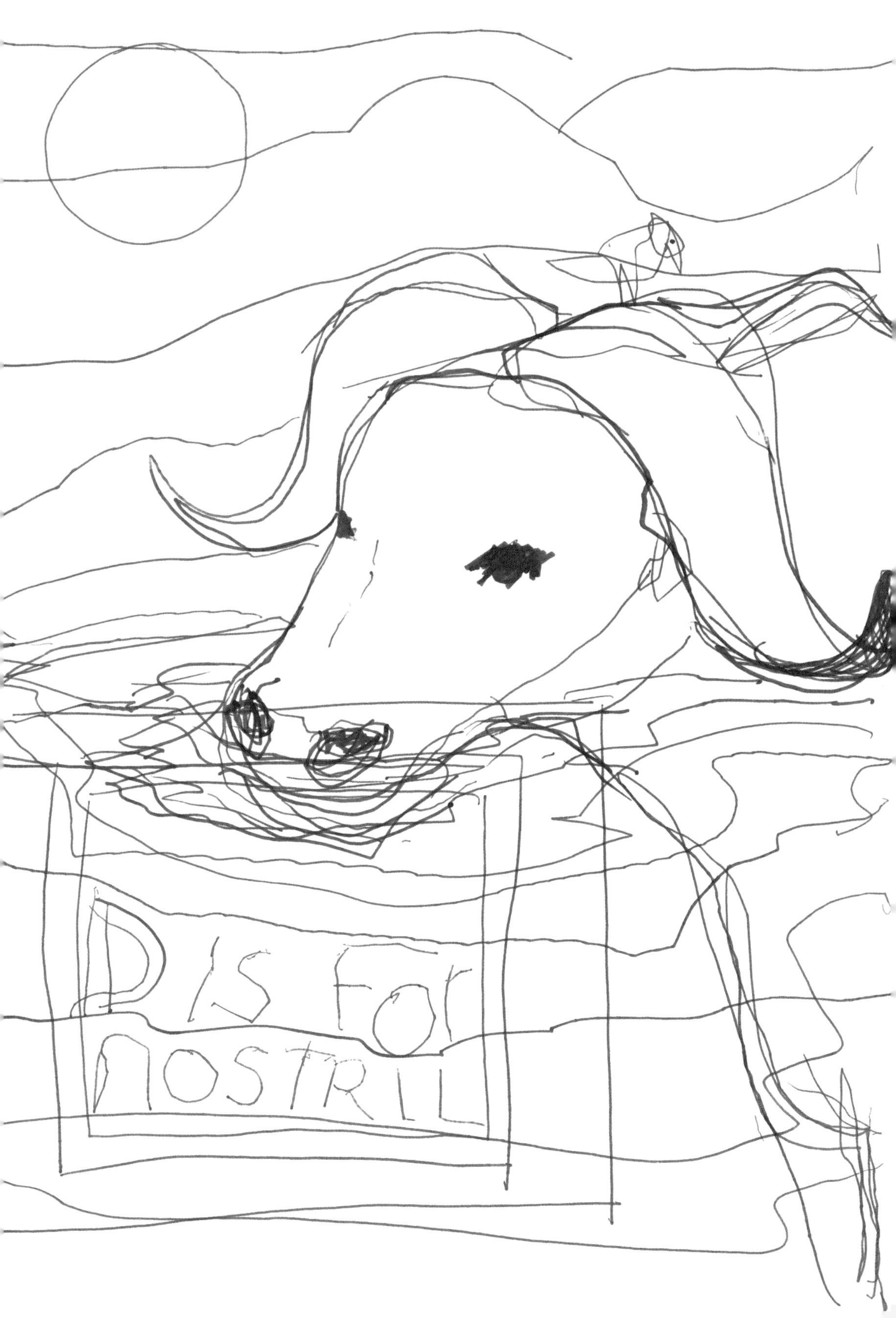
N is For
nostril

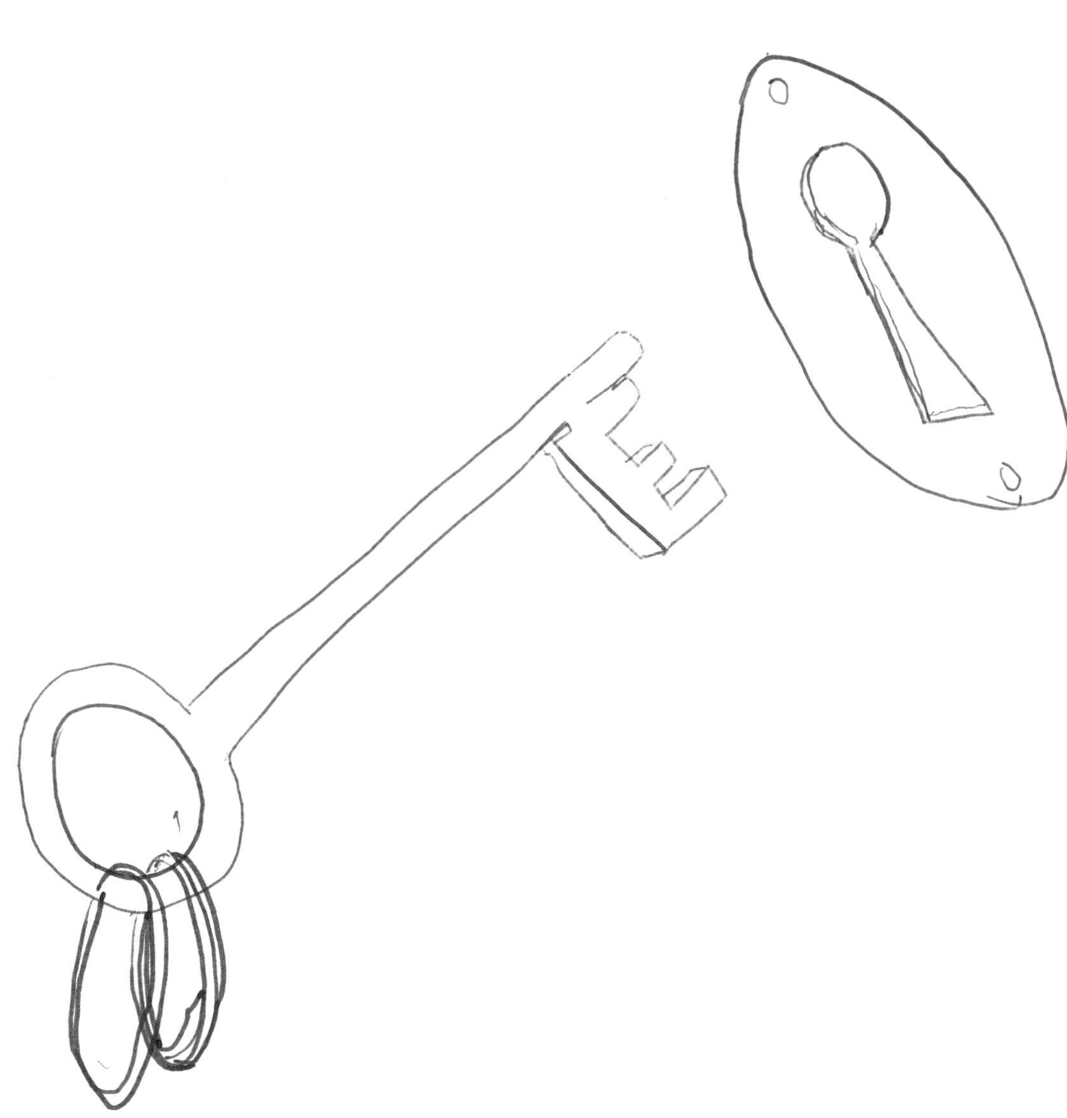

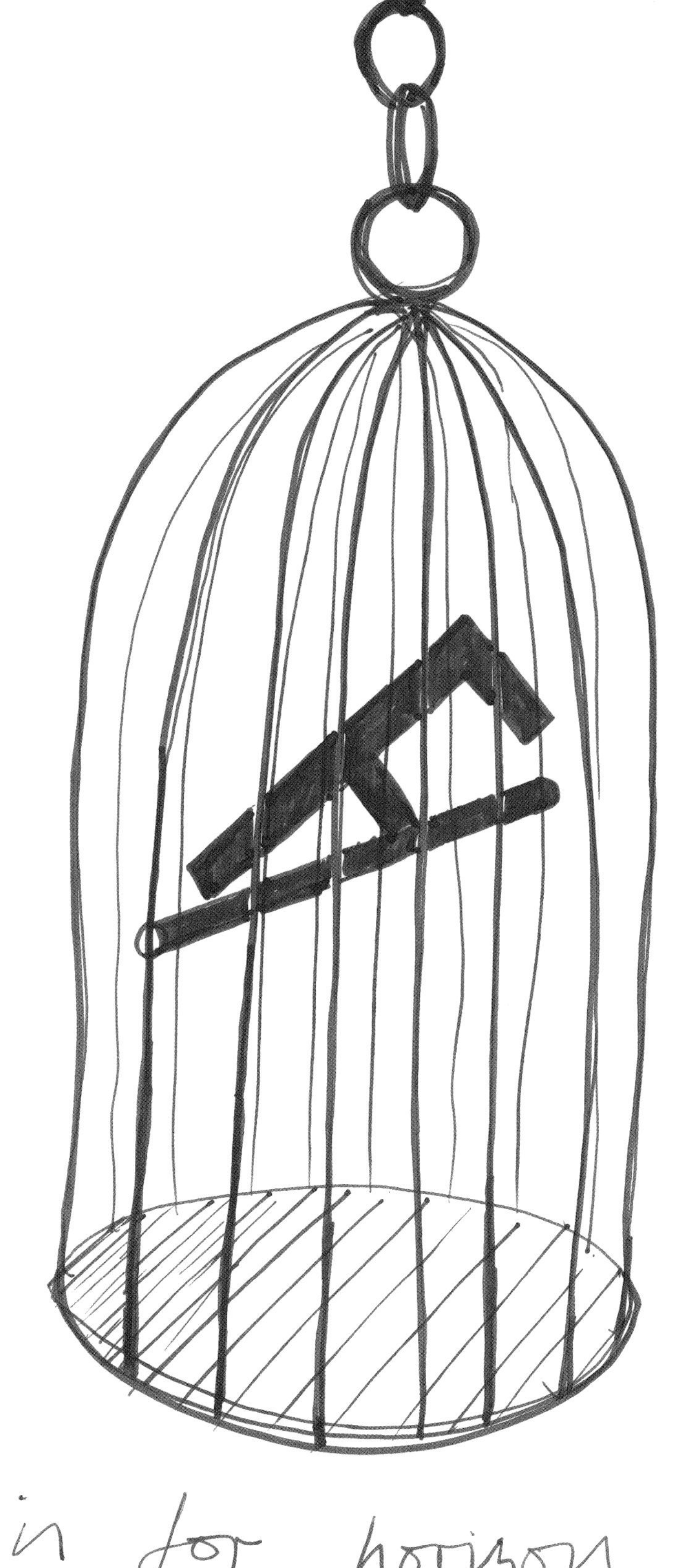

in for horizon

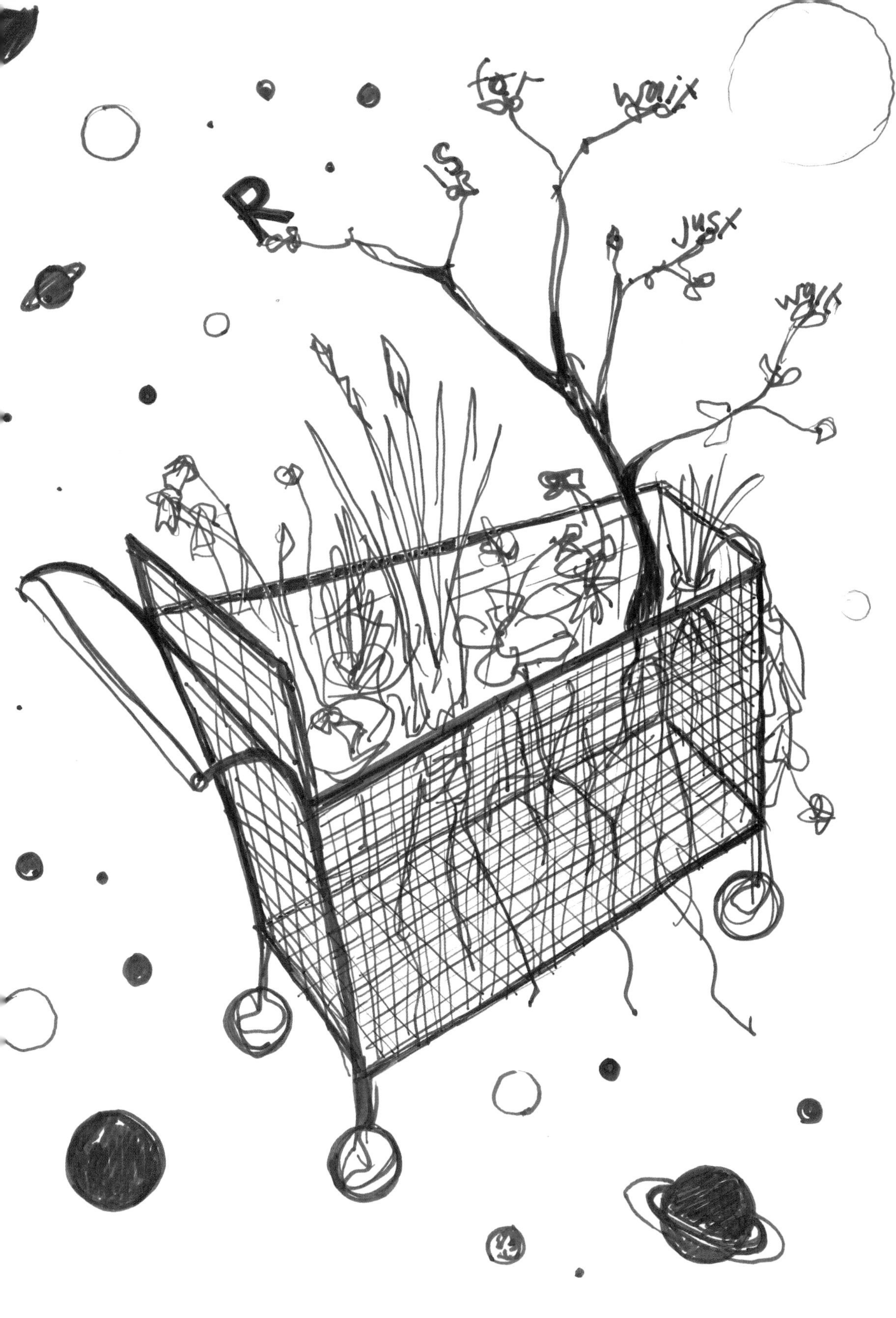

R
is
for
wait
just
wait
wait

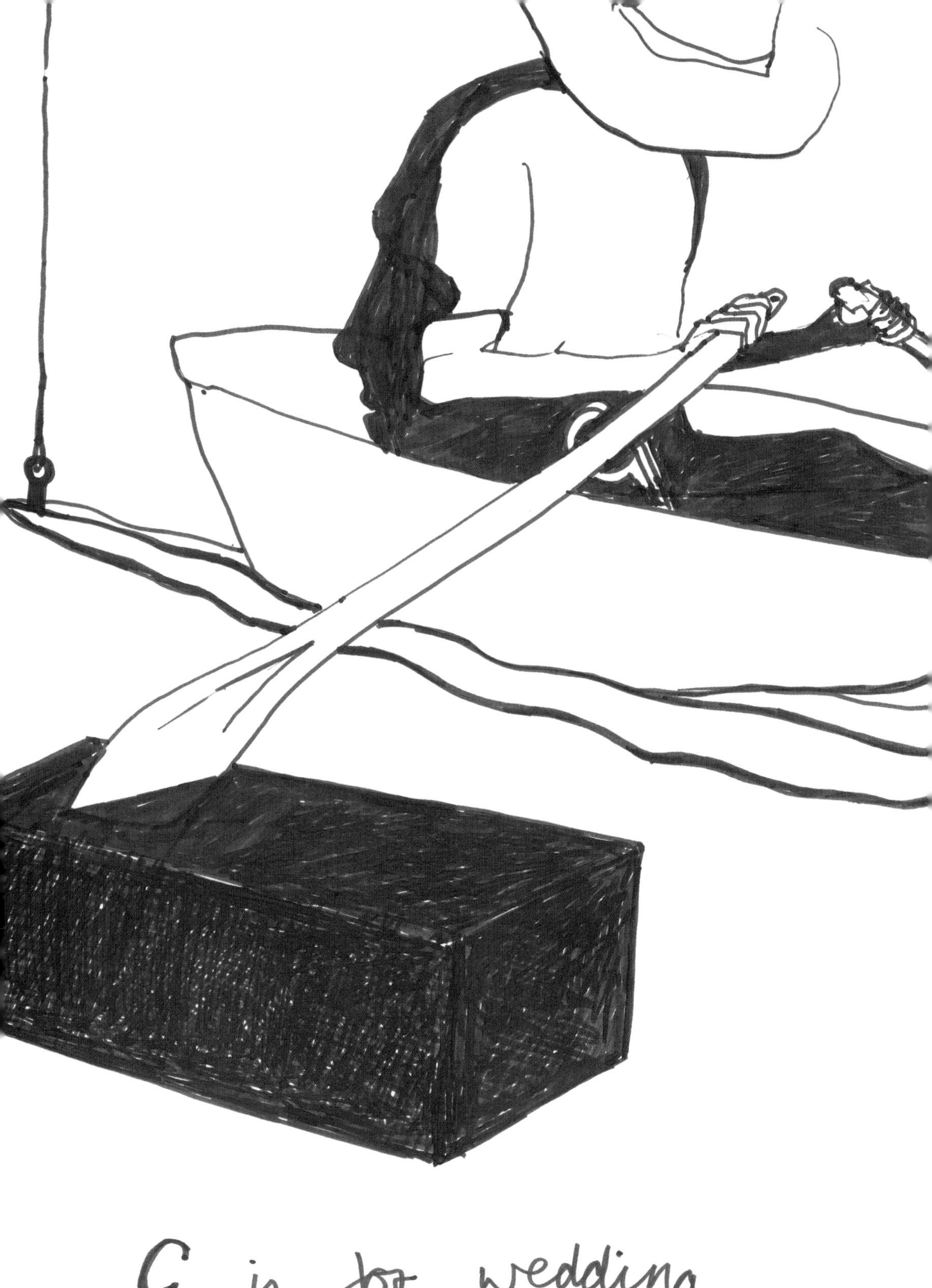

G is for wedding

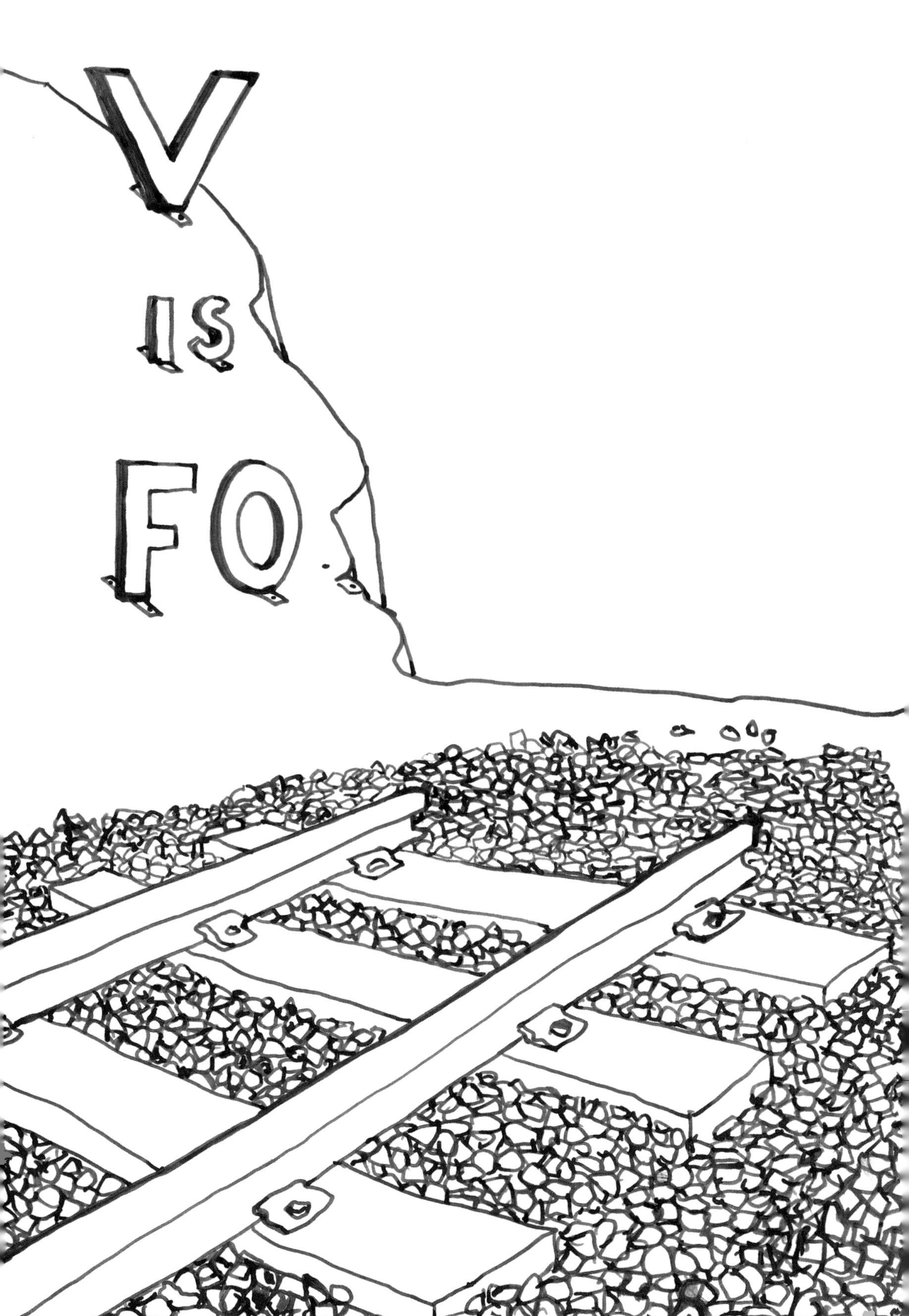
V
IS
FO

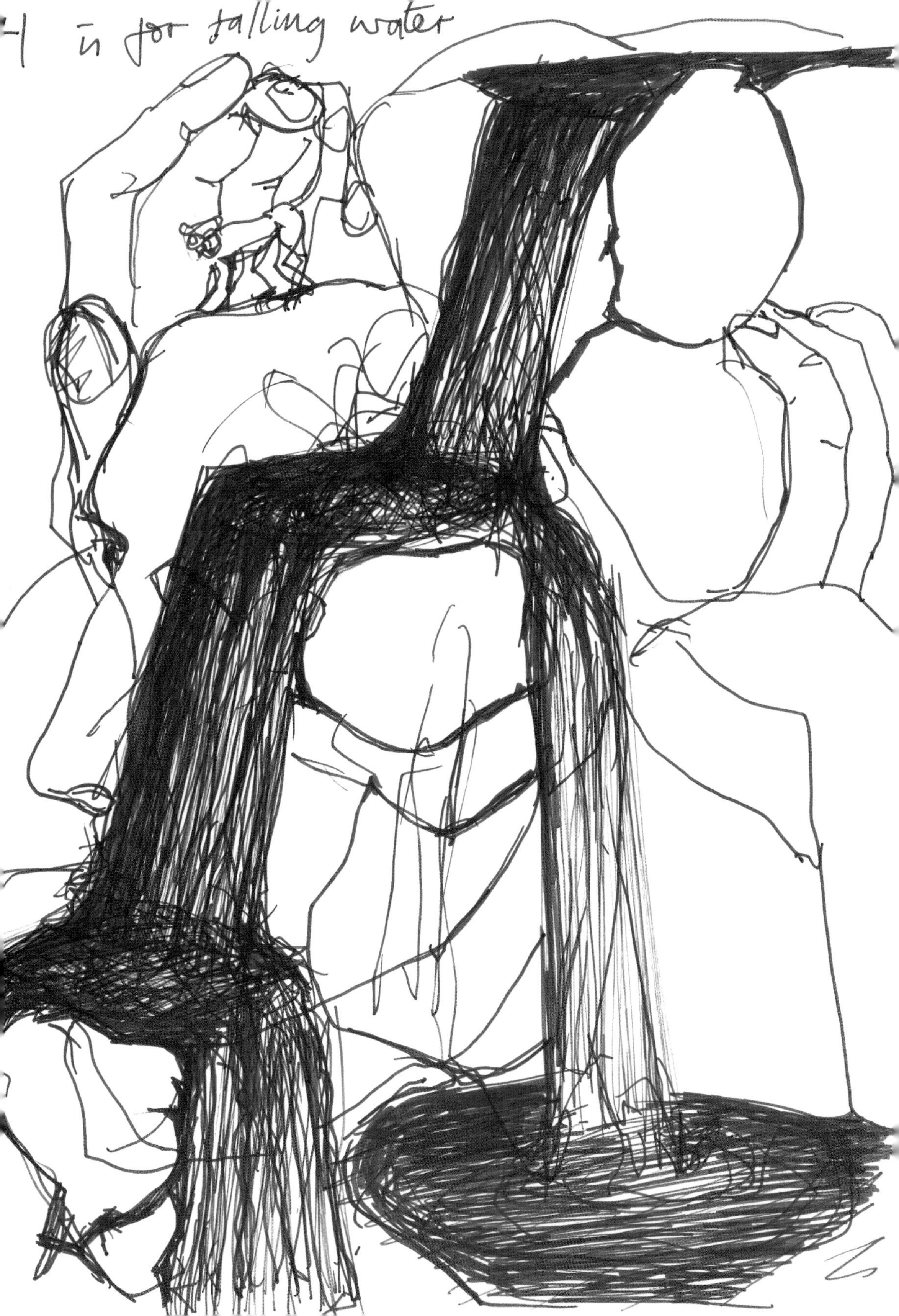
H is for falling water

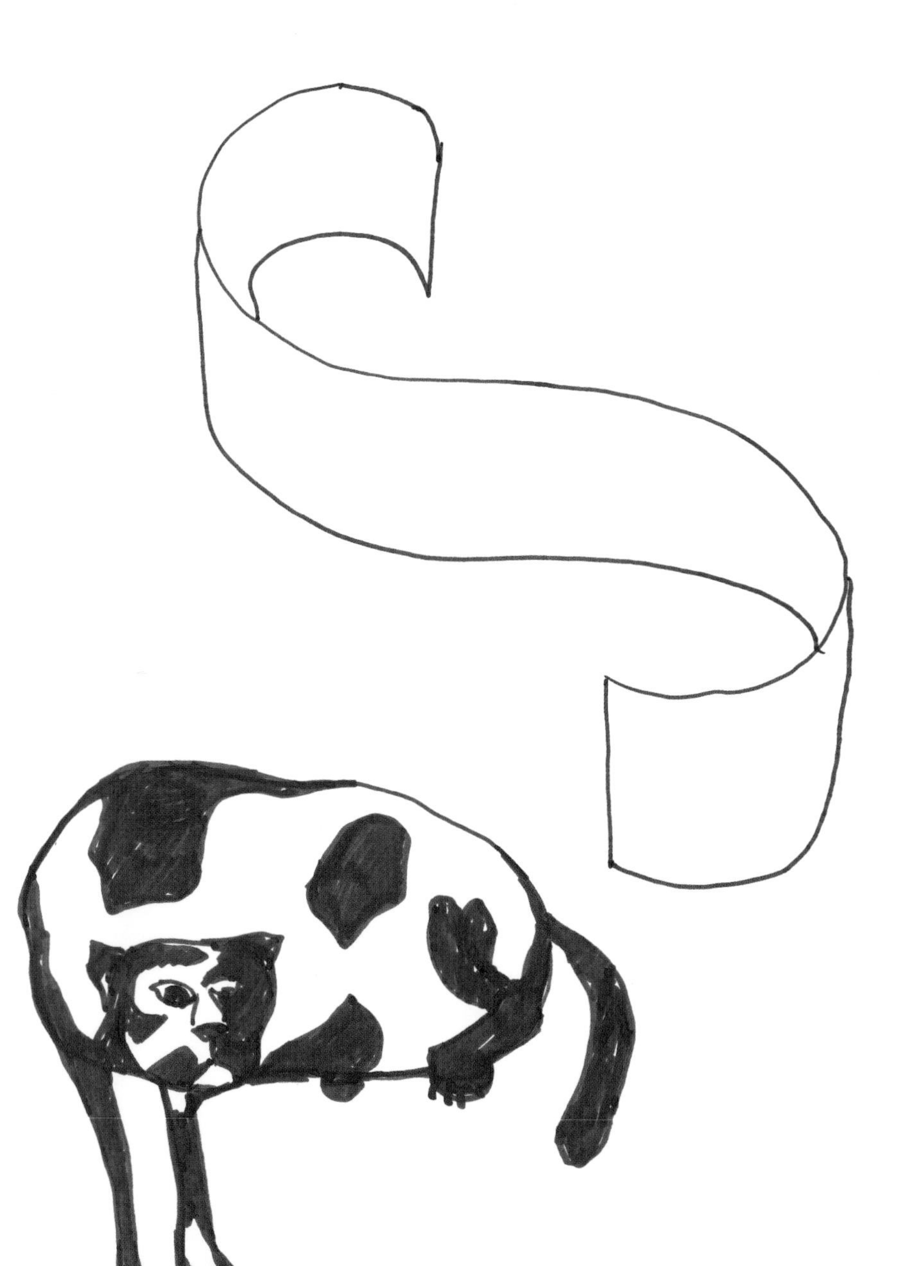

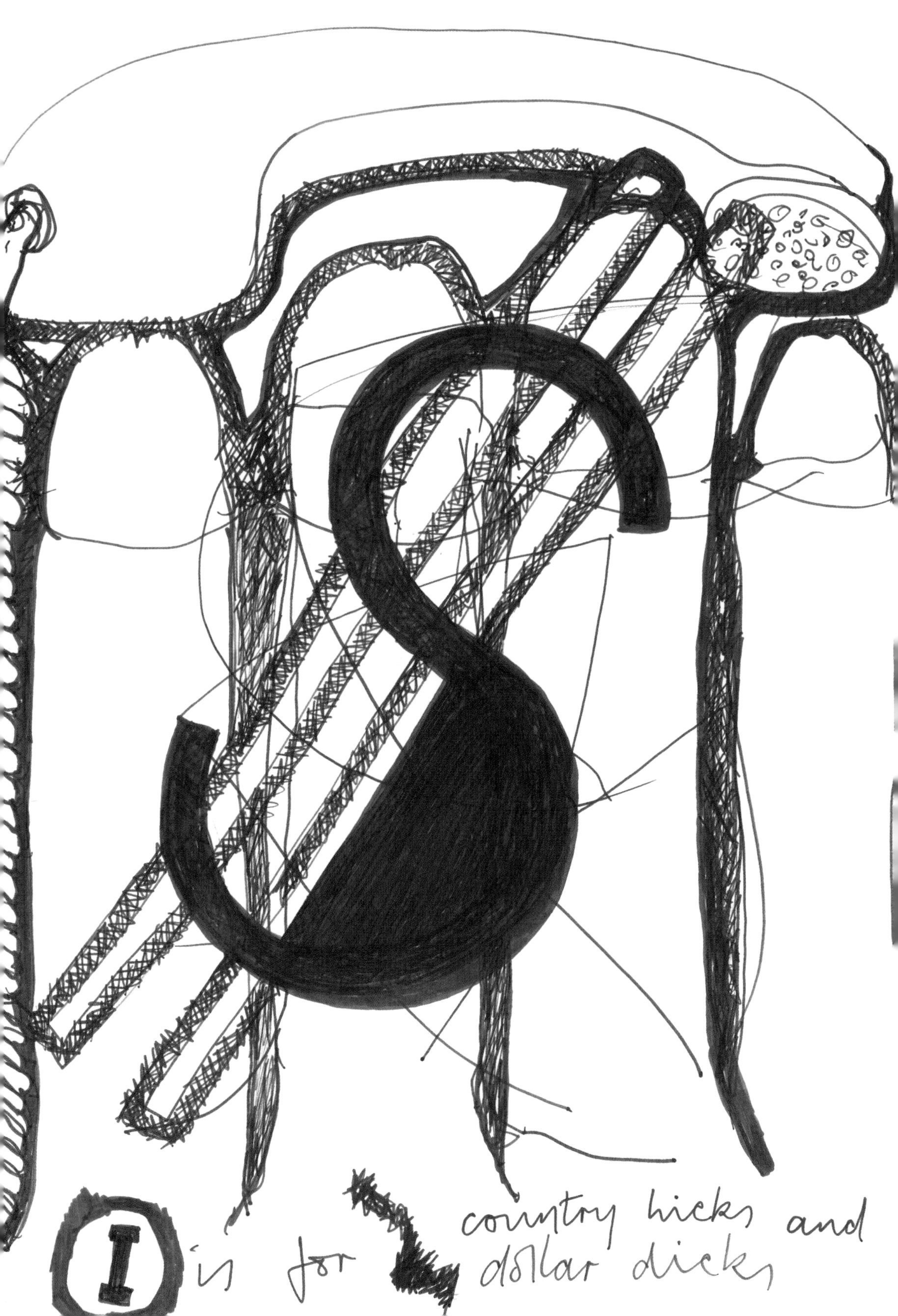
I
'is for   country hicks and
dollar dicks

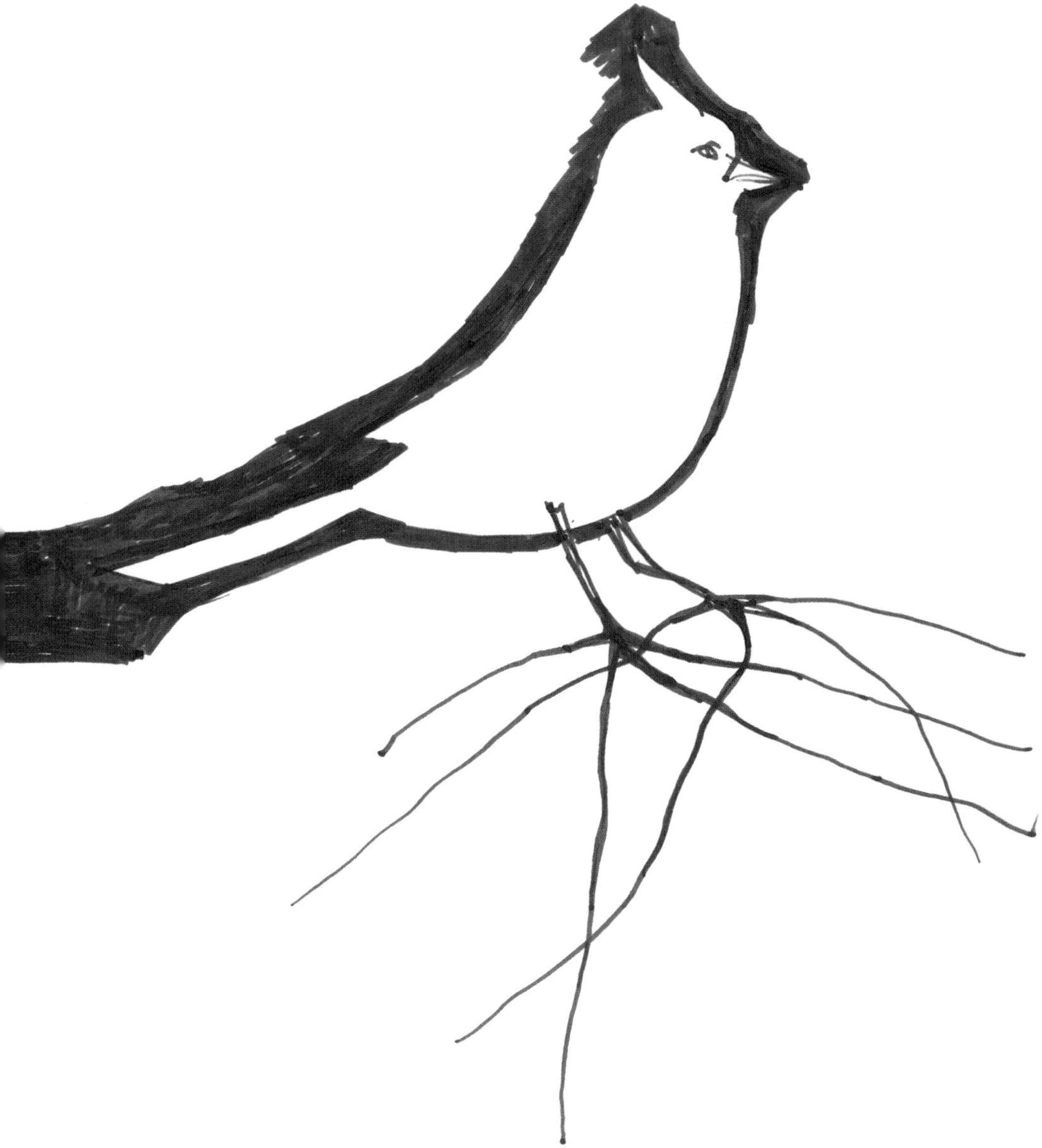

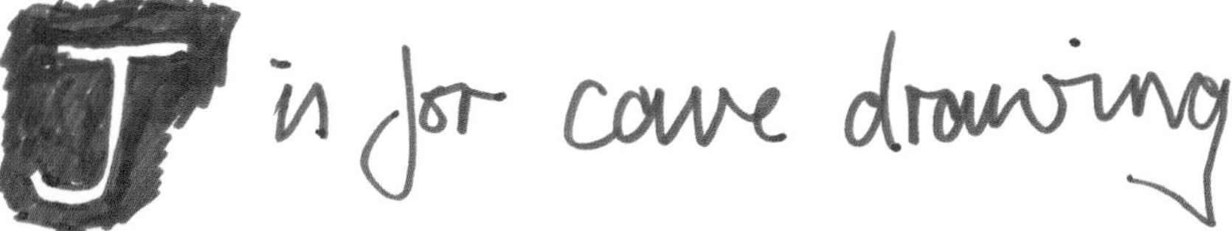
is for cave drawing

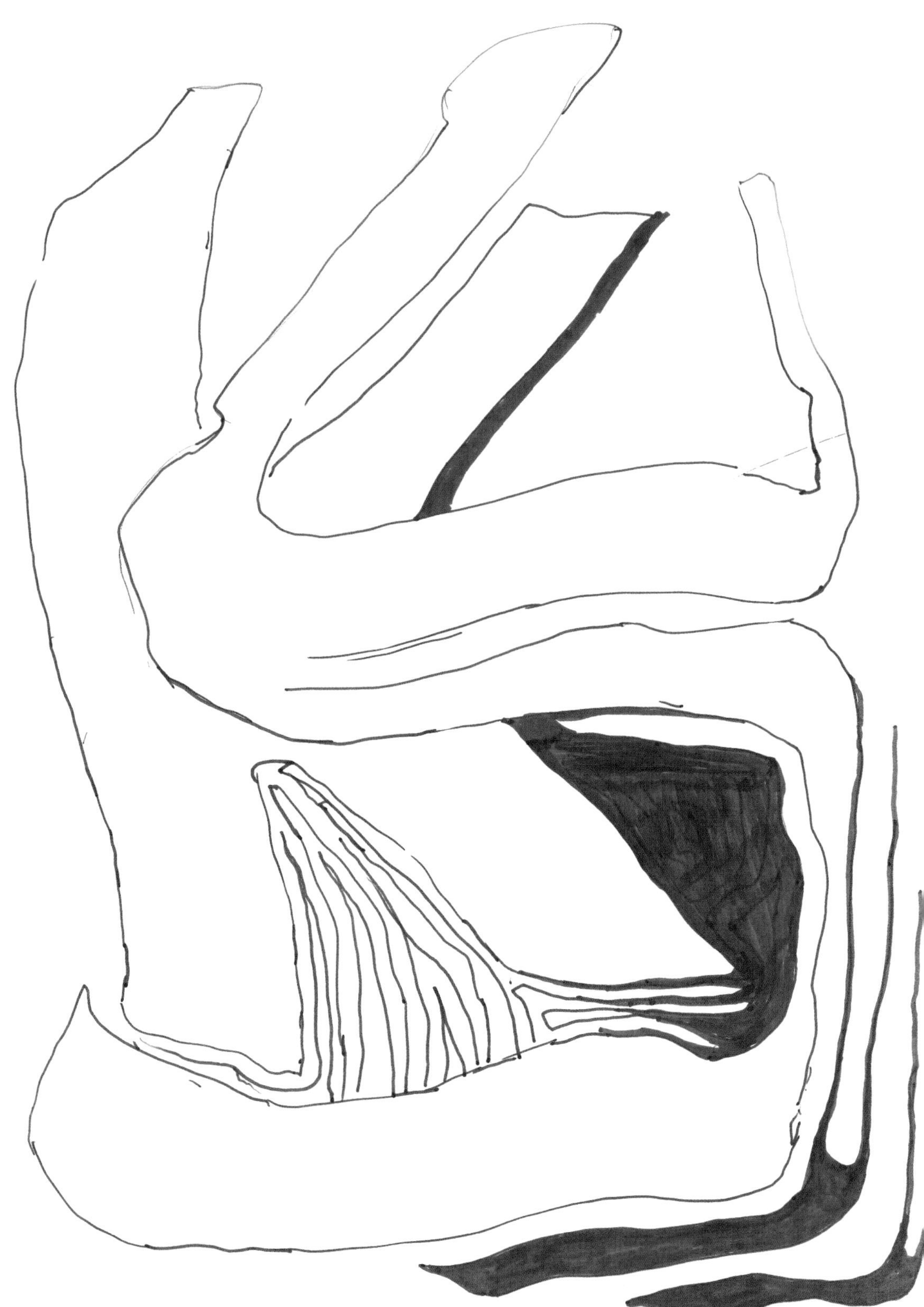

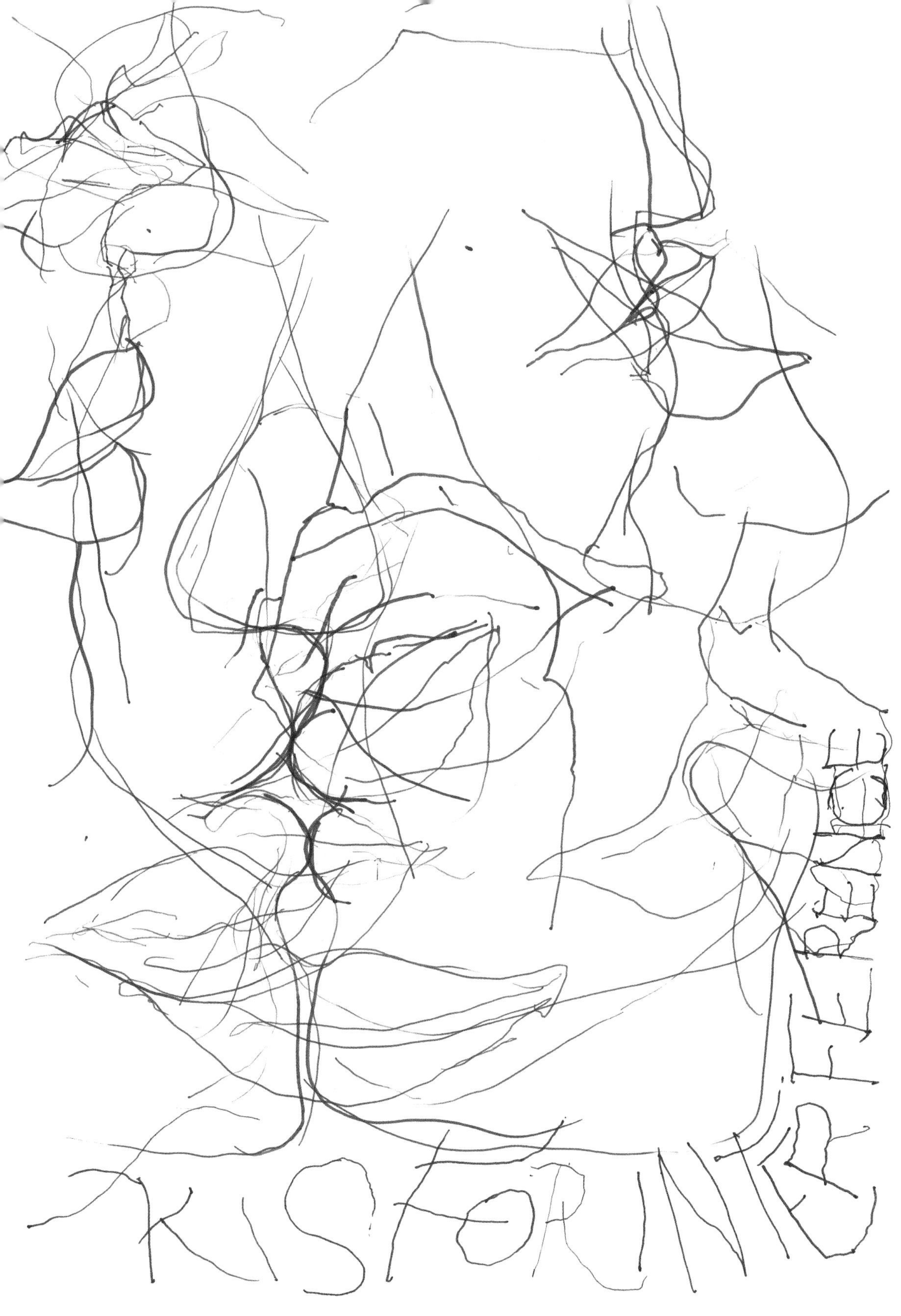

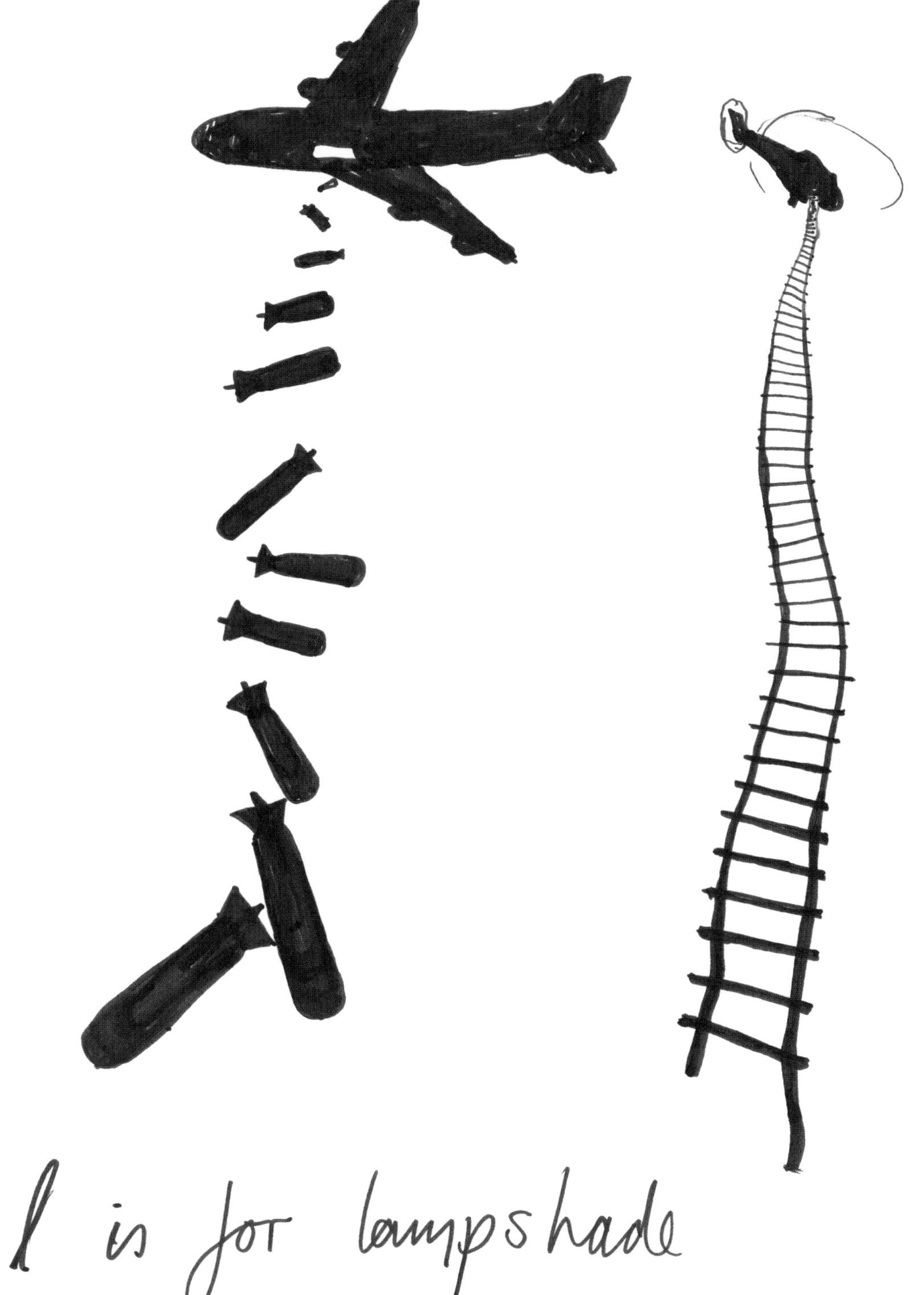

l is for lampshade

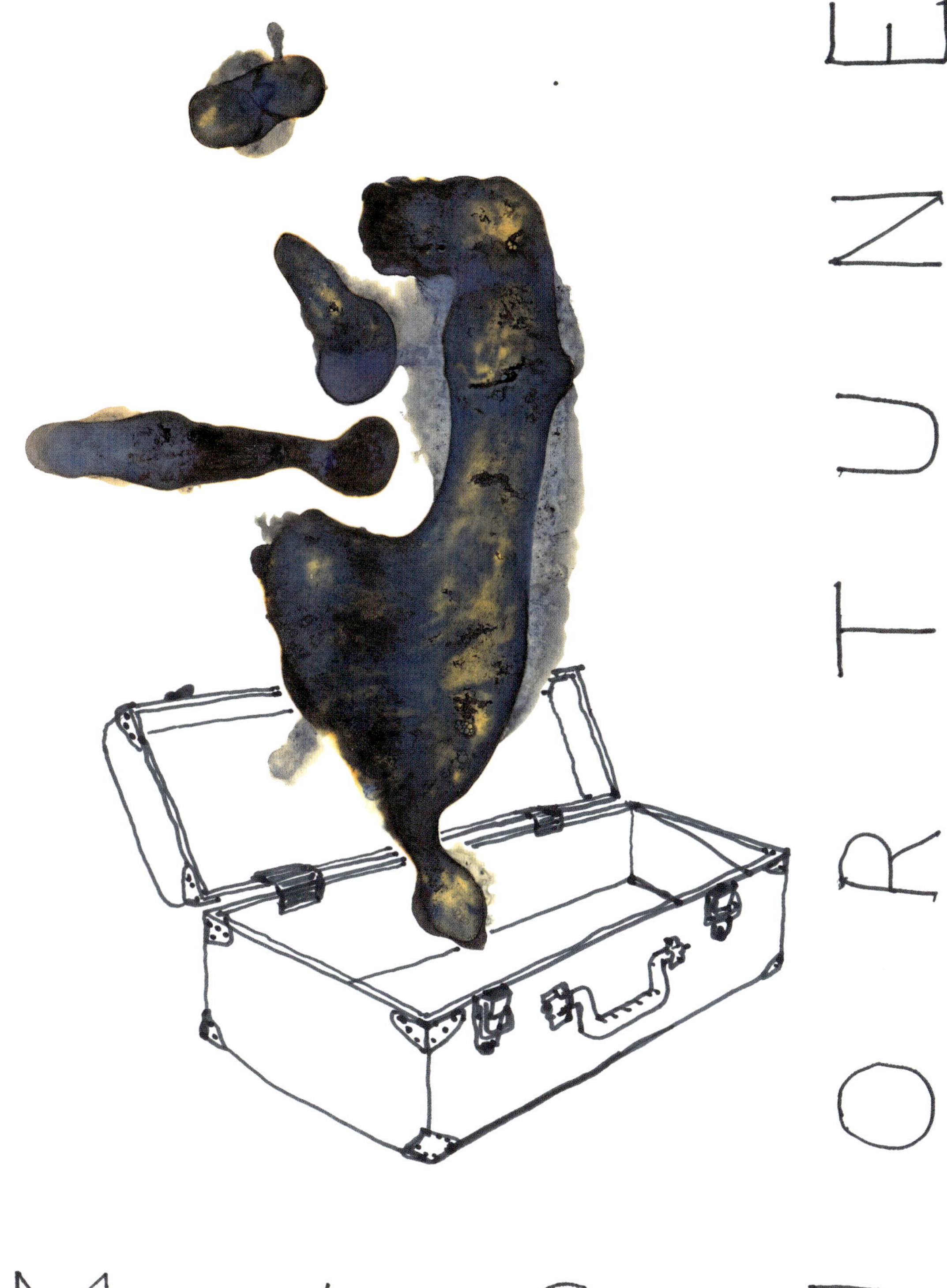
MISFORTUNE

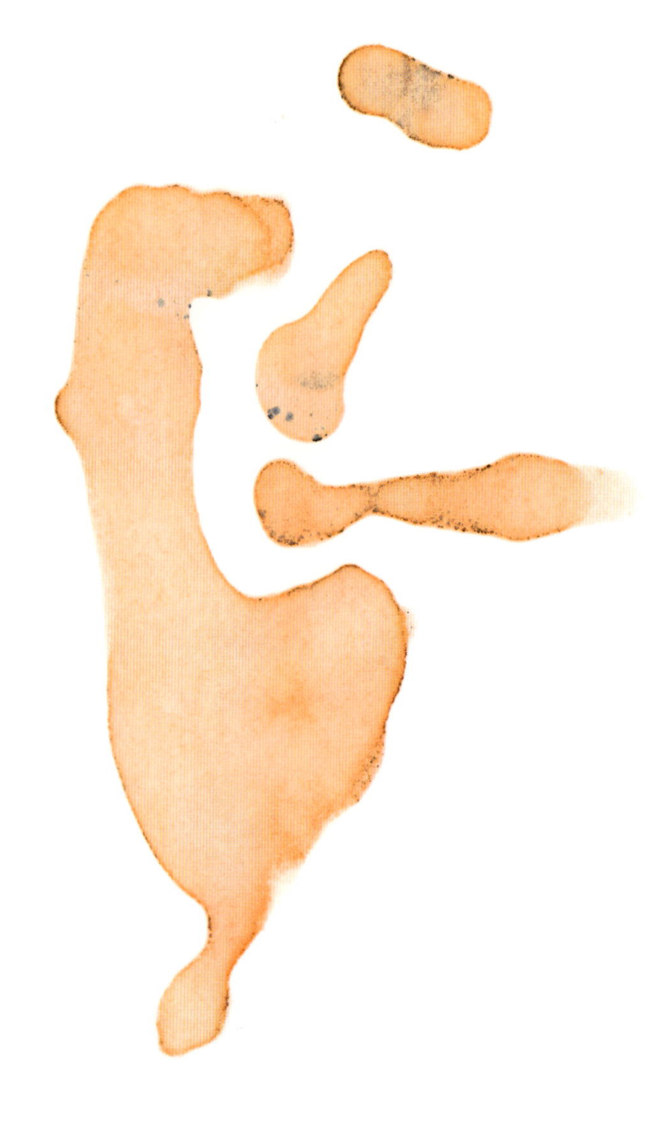

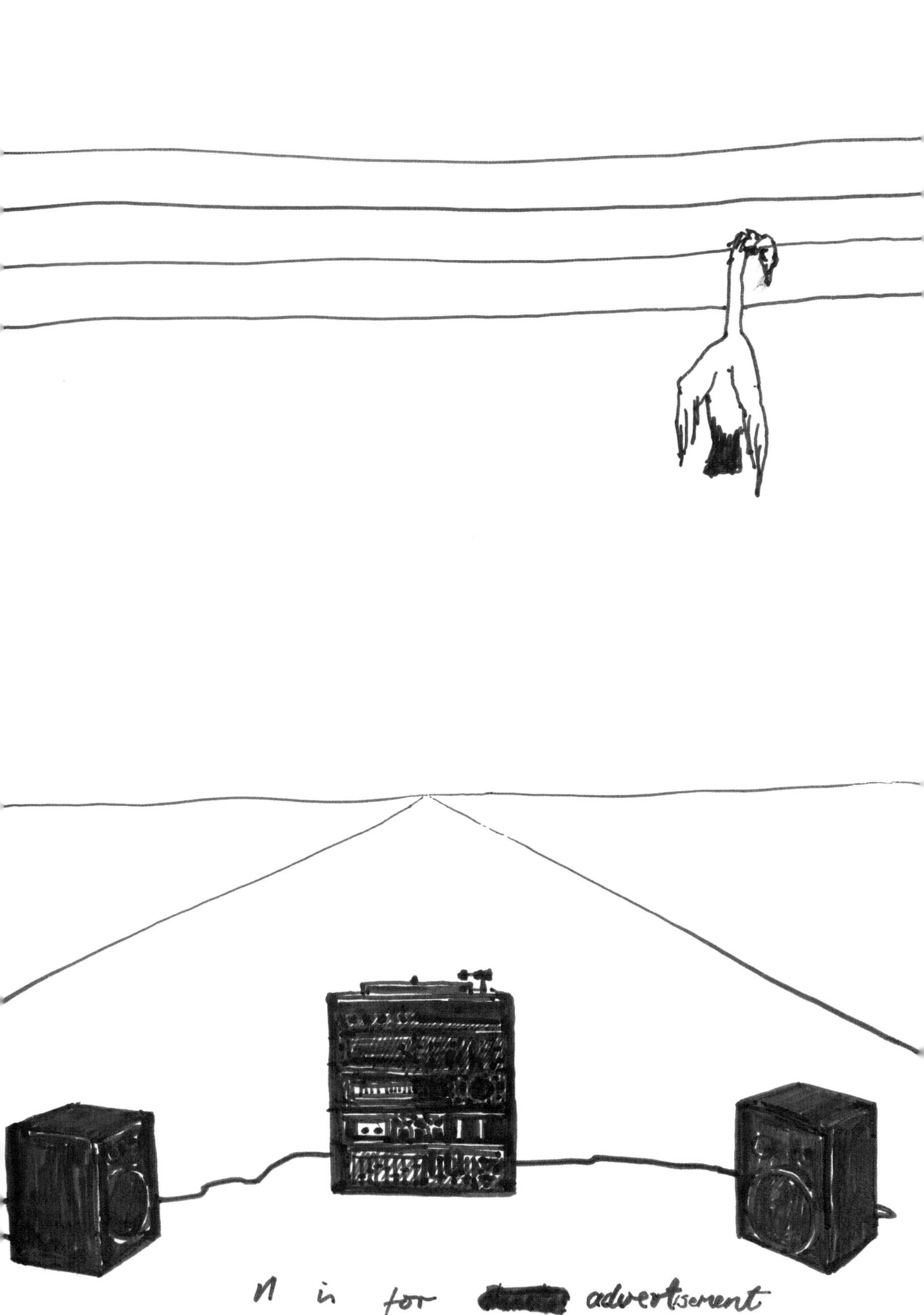

N is for ~~advert~~ advertisement

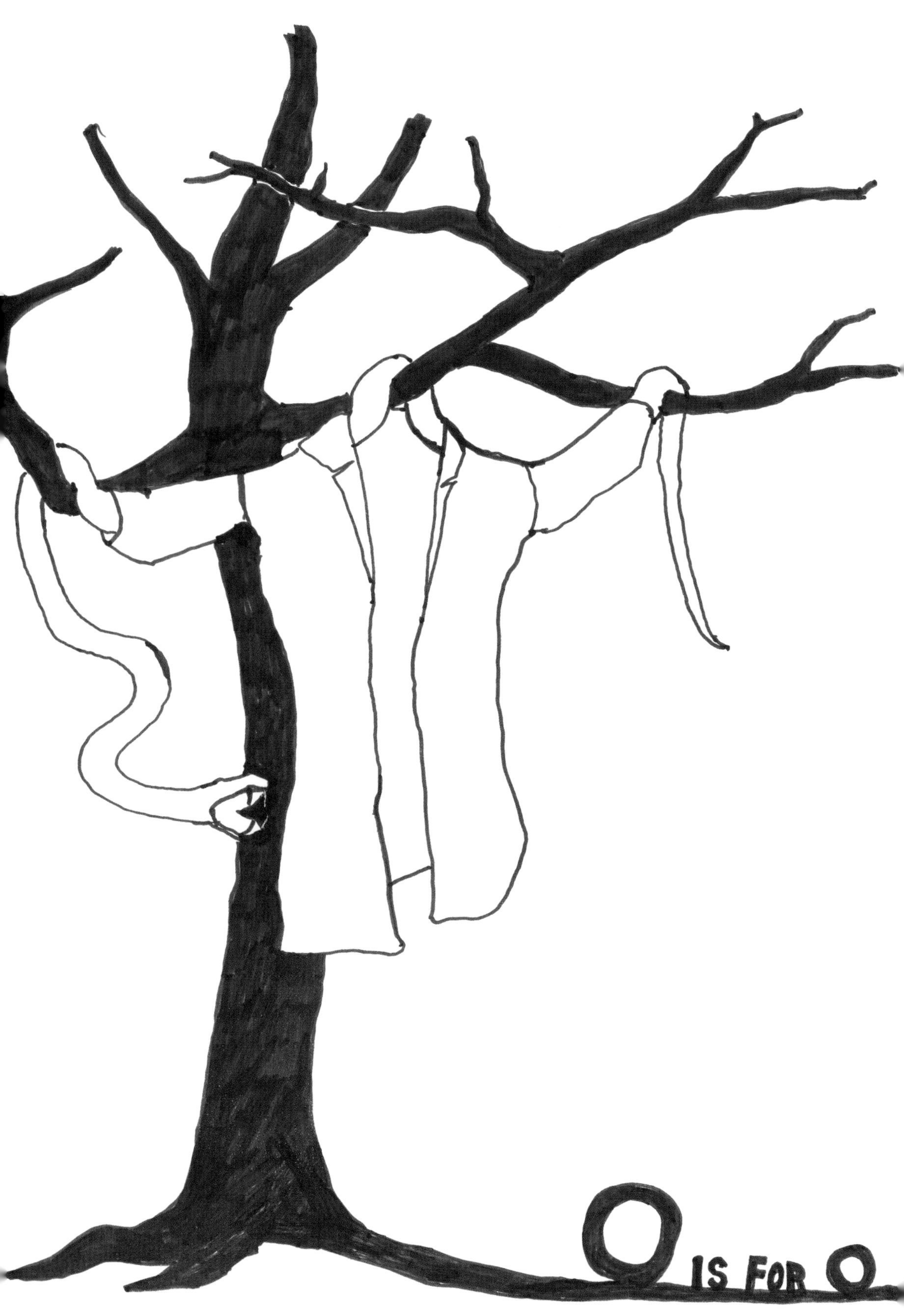
O IS FOR O

P is for the wonderfull world of great moti
PEACE

Q is for black and white or colour

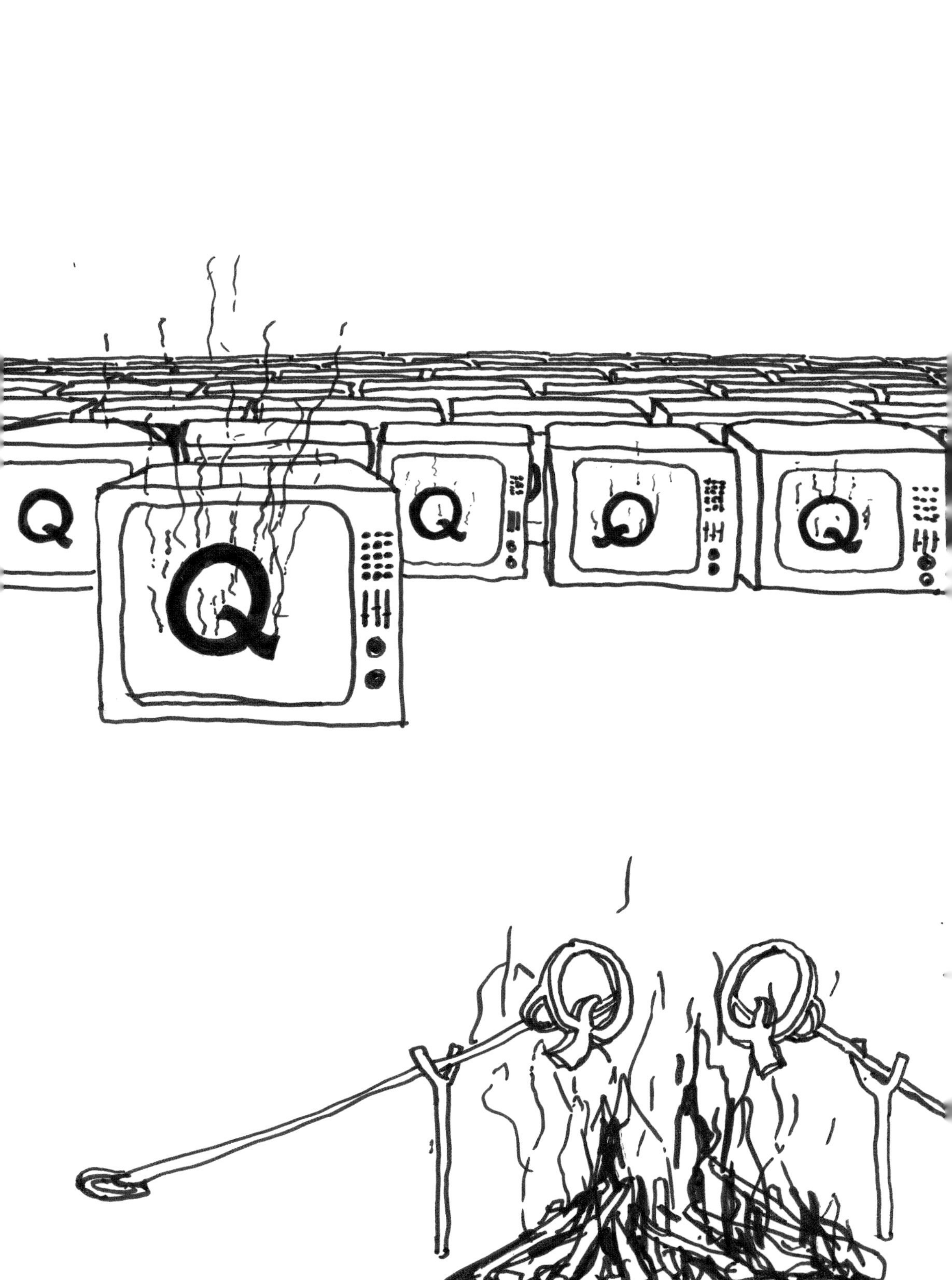

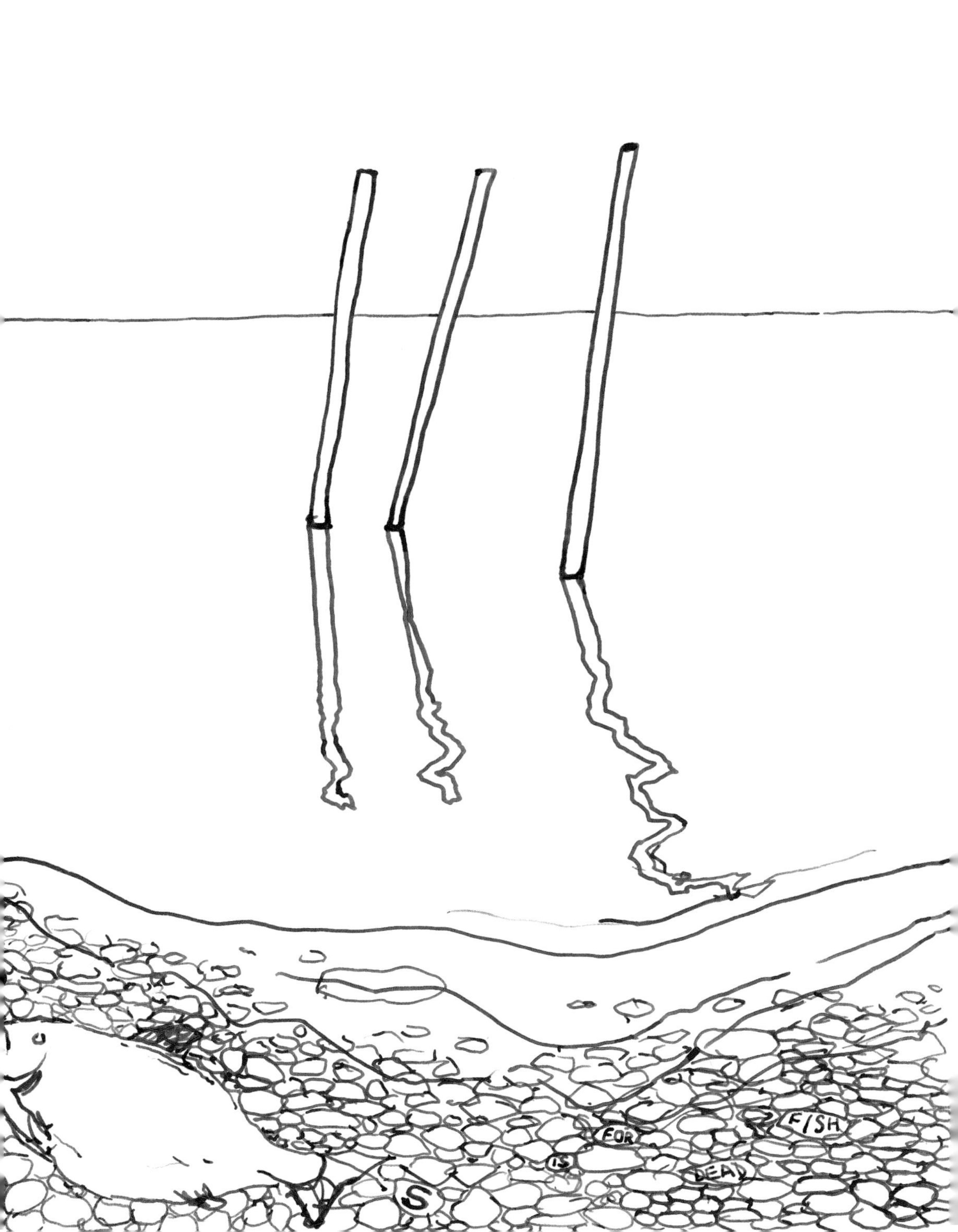
S
IS
FOR
DEAD
FISH

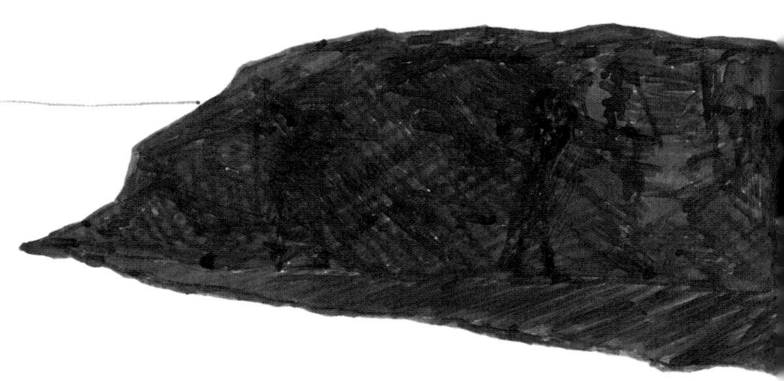
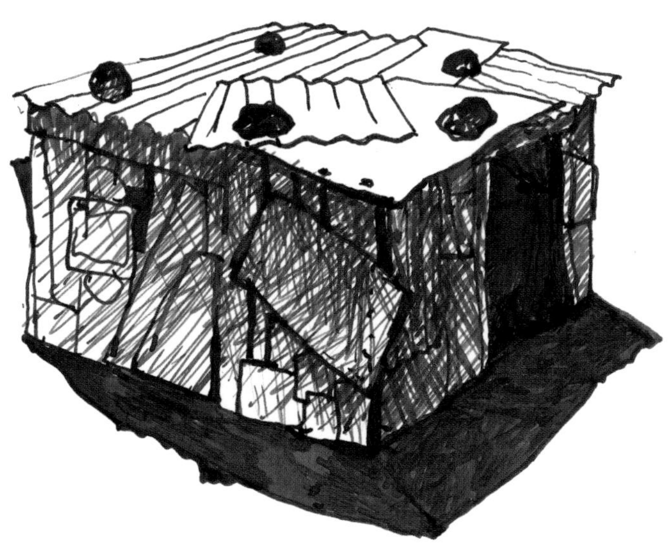
T
IS FOR
LEARNING
TO READ OR

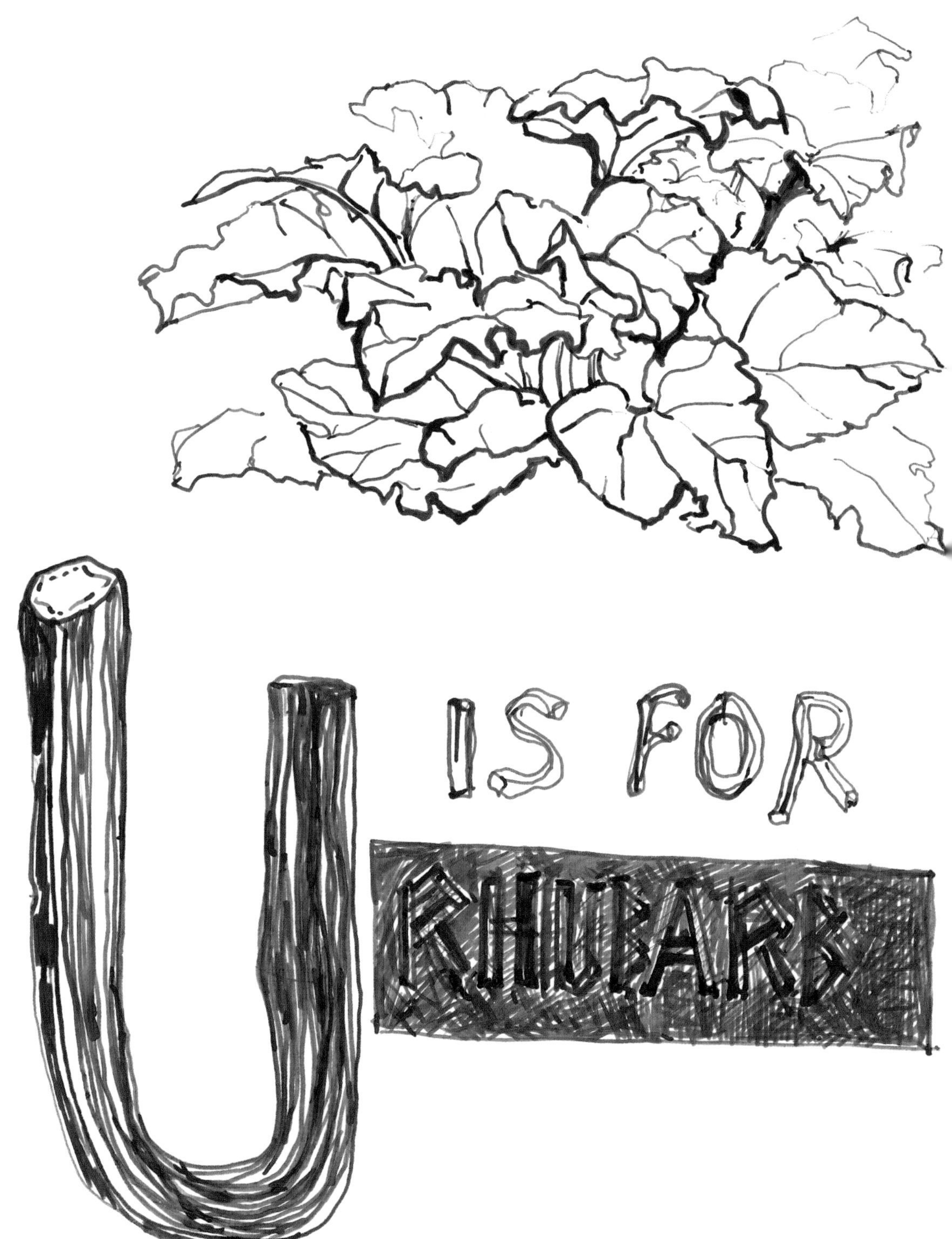
U
IS FOR
RHUBARB

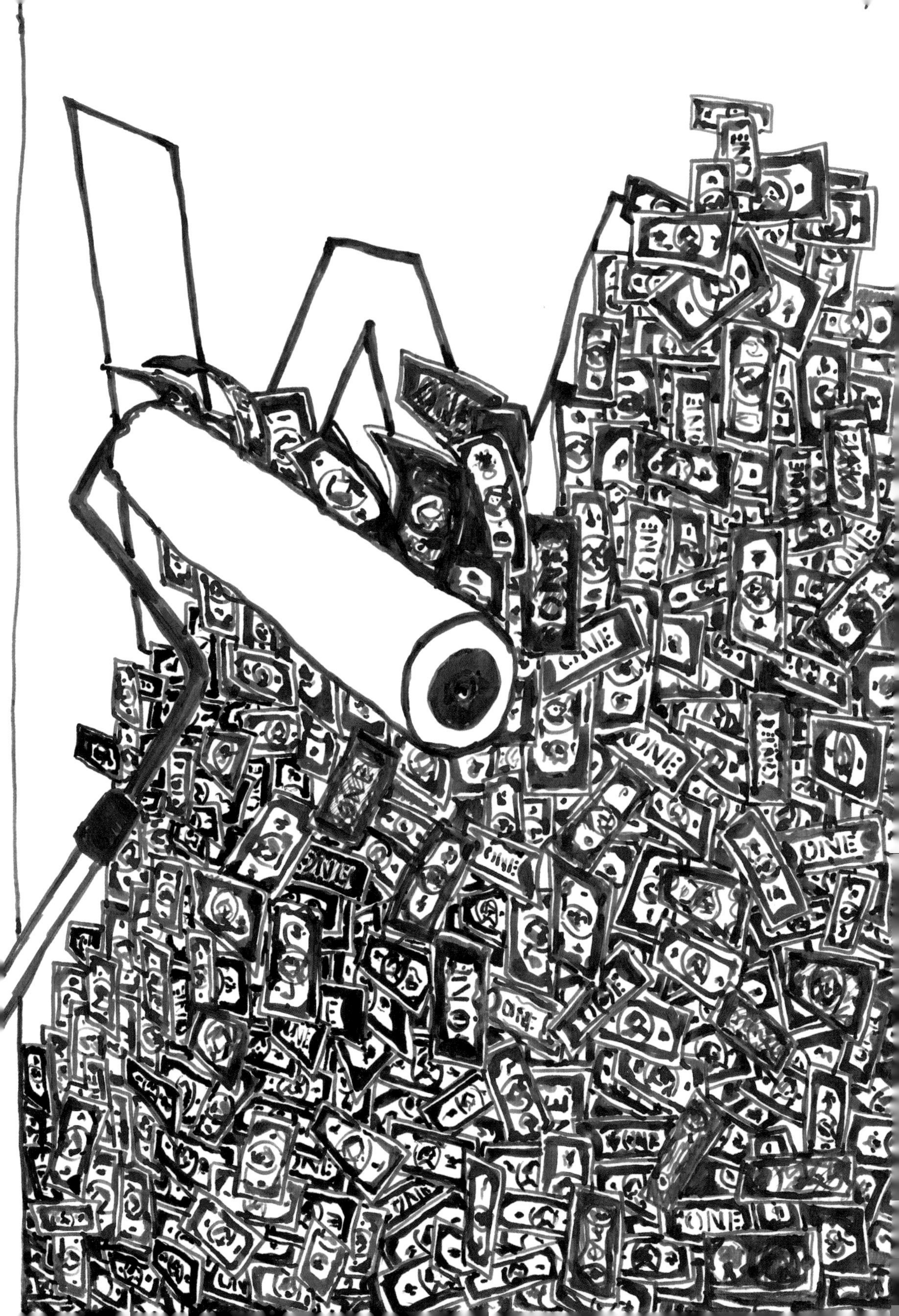

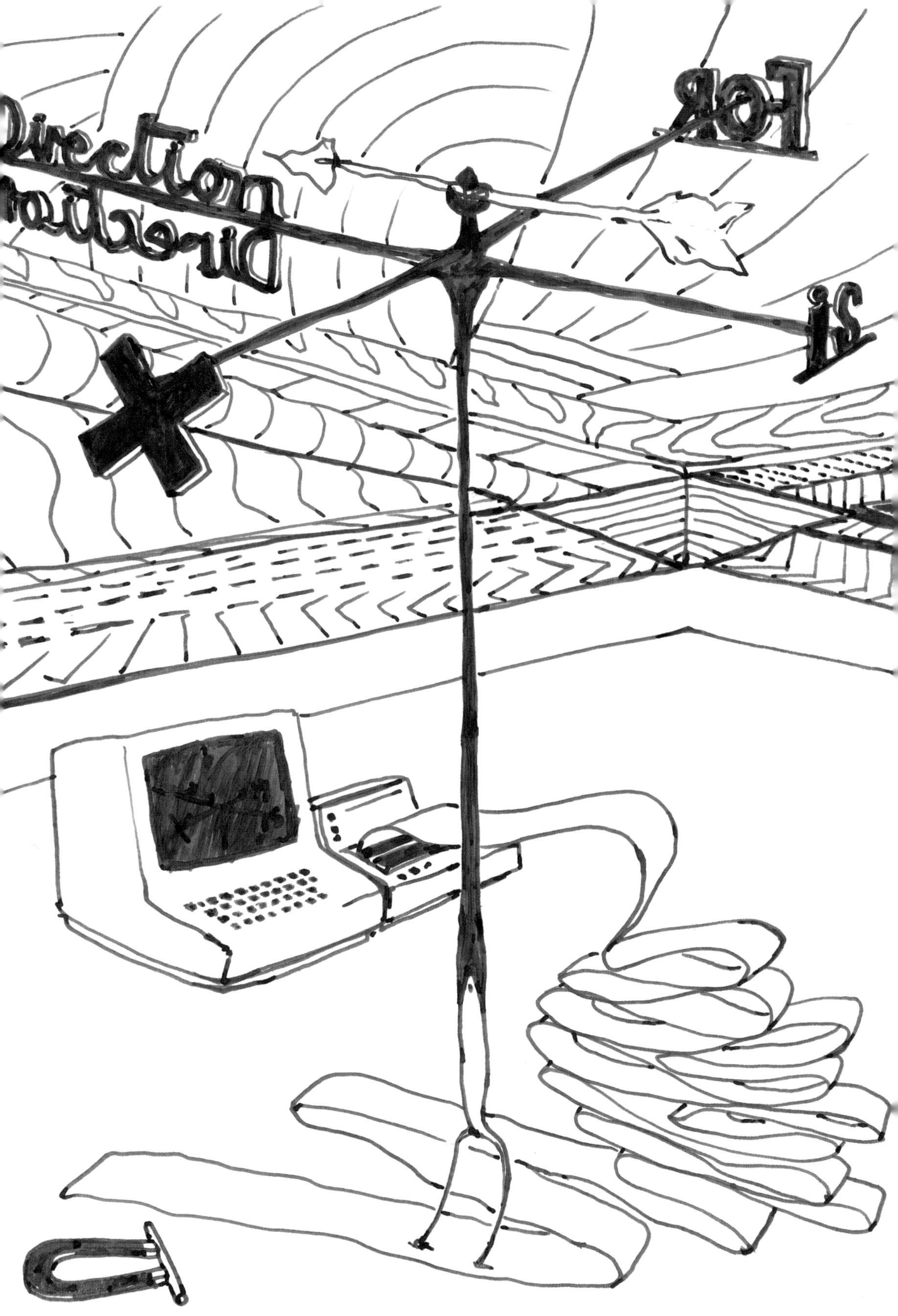

For
is
Direction
Direction

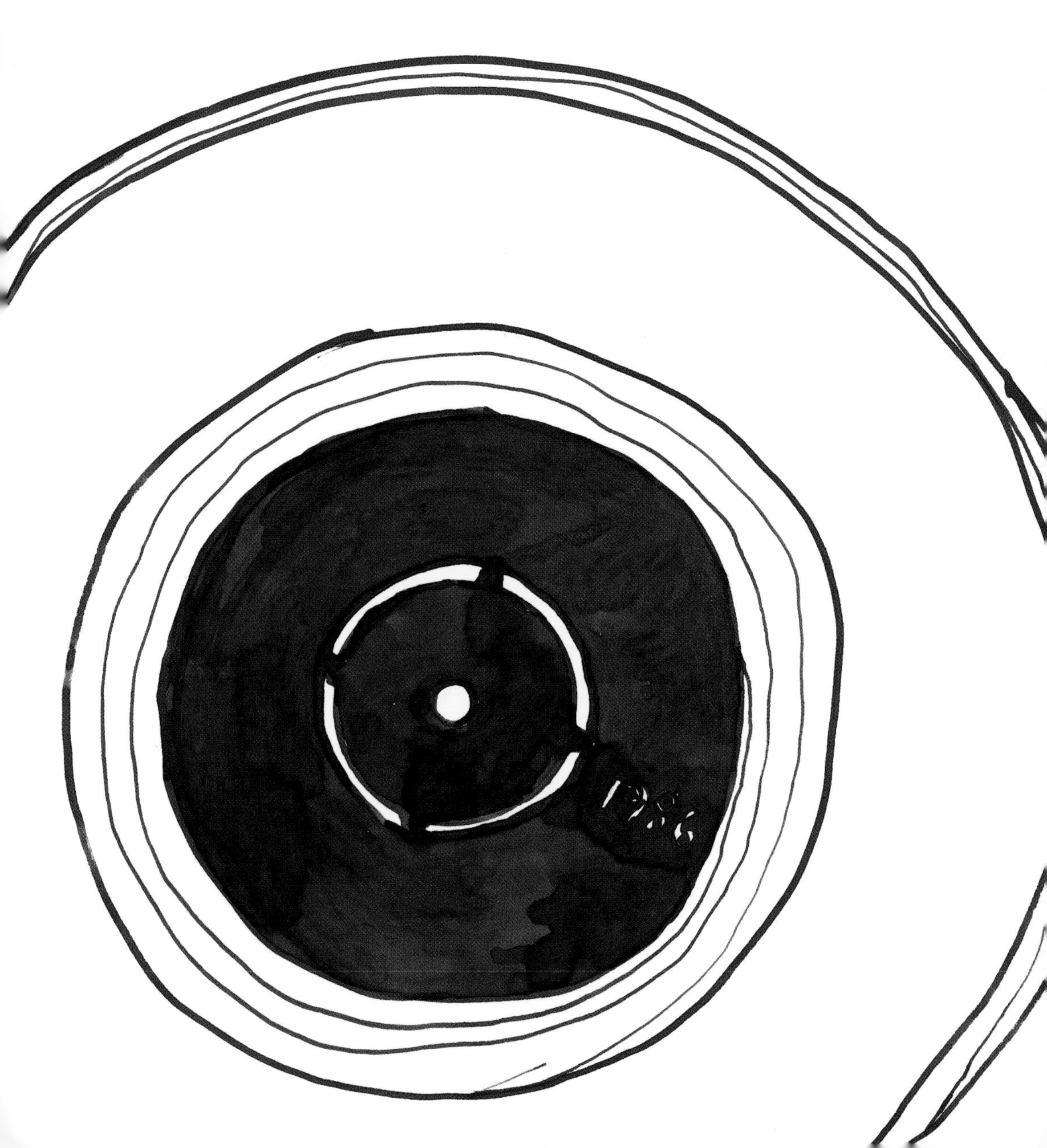

1986

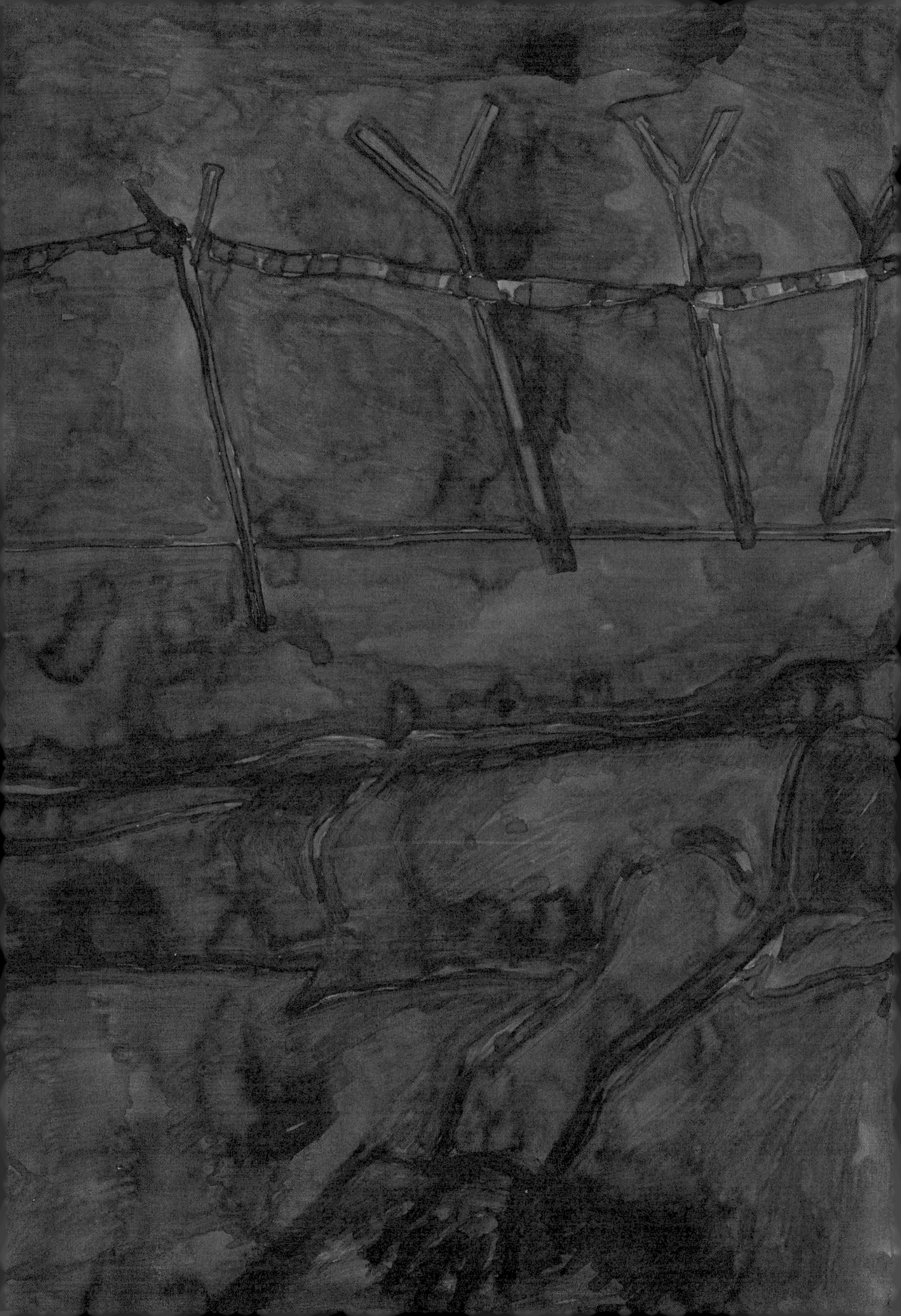

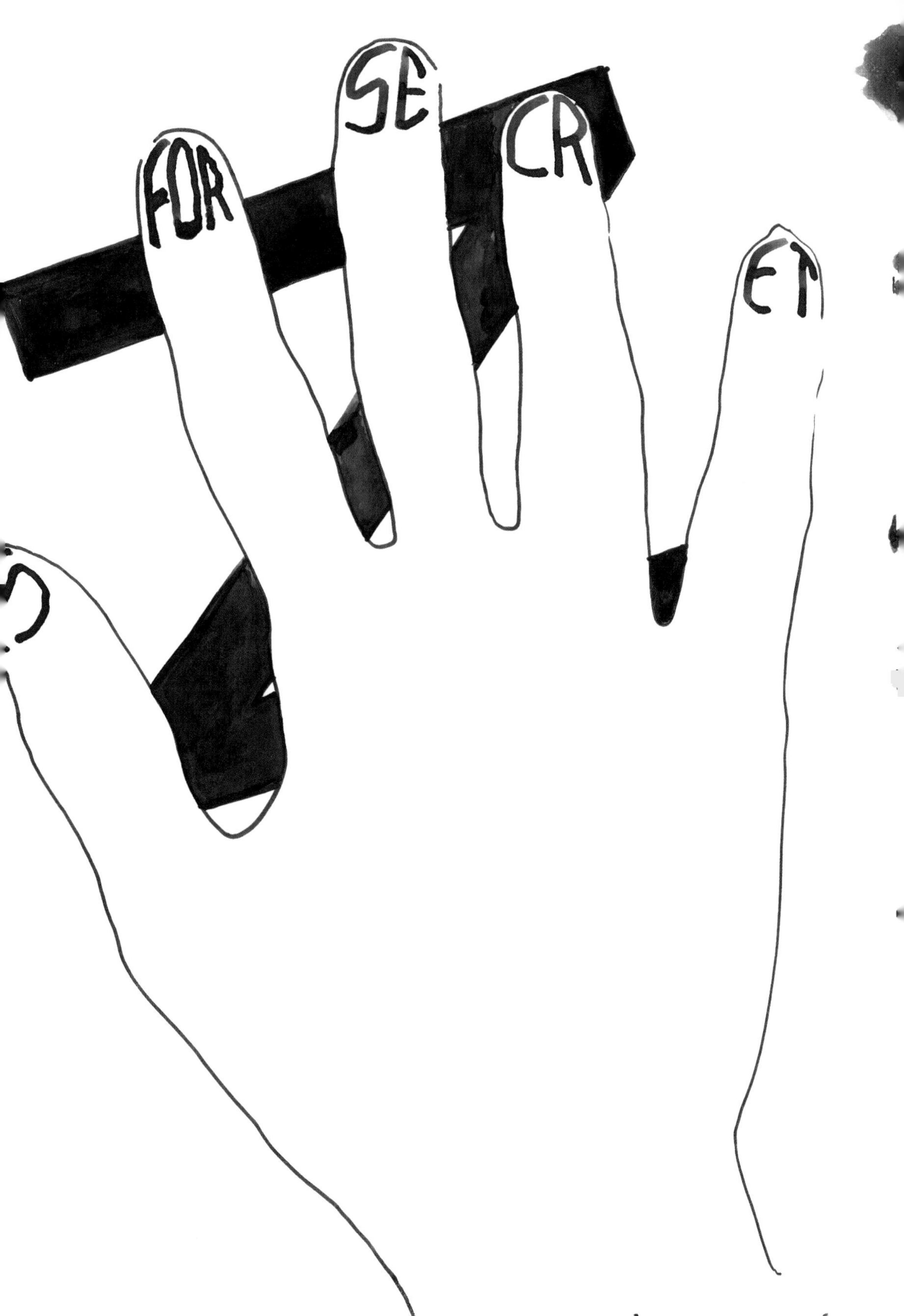
FOR
SE
CR
ET

ALPHABET by Bill Woodrow RA
is a facsimile of a book
of drawings made in 1986

Royal Academy Publications
Beatrice Gullström
Alison Hissey
Elizabeth Horne
Carola Krueger
Peter Sawbridge
Nick Tite

Design
Kathrin Jacobsen

**Photography and
colour origination**
John Bodkin/DawkinsColour

Printed in Wales
by Gomer Press Limited

British Library Cataloguing-
in-Publication Data
A catalogue record for this book
is available from the British Library

ISBN 978-1-907533-83-9

Distributed outside the
United States and Canada
by Thames & Hudson Ltd,
London

Distributed in the
United States and Canada
by Harry N. Abrams, Inc.,
New York

Born in 1948 near Henley in Oxfordshire,
Bill Woodrow RA studied at Winchester School
of Art, and in London at St Martin's School
of Art and Chelsea School of Art. By the early
1980s, when the first of his celebrated 'cut-out'
sculptural works appeared, his reputation
was firmly established. Woodrow's constant
expressions of irony, loss and humour,
his examination of the human condition
and modern society, and the range of his
differing processes and materials, all skilfully
employed, have ensured that his work has
remained consistently challenging and
fascinating over the five decades of his
career to date. He was a finalist for the
Turner Prize in 1986, was one of three artists
chosen to make a sculpture for the fourth plinth
in Trafalgar Square in 2000, and was elected
a Royal Academician in 2002. He lives and
works in London and Hampshire.